Inspiring Words to Rhyme

A personal touch from GOD

Inspiring Words to Rhyme

A personal touch from GOD

Judy C. Boggs

FARMHOUSE PUBLISHERS

HEBRON, KENTUCKY

Printed in the United States of America

First Printing 2014

ISBN: 978-0692225226

Farmhouse Publishers, LLC
2155 Lumberjack Drive
Hebron, Kentucky 41048

www.farmhousepublishers.com

This book is lovingly dedicated to
Tim.
His full love and support made
this endeavor a pure joy and blessing.

───────────────────────

ℭℬ

"Husbands, love your wives, just as Christ loved the church
and gave himself up for her."

Ephesians 5:25

CONTENTS

ACKNOWLEDGMENTS

*F*irst of all, let me give praise to the source of my inspiration. Without the love of Jesus and the Holy Spirit, and without the guidance of God my Heavenly Father, there would be no words to write down. All glory and honor is due unto the One who gives my heart the peace to write, the joy to sing, and the reason to express.

Let me say next that I could not have written this book without the constant love and encouragement I received from my husband Tim. He is my helpmeet and a most faithful man of God. We love serving together, with God being number one in our lives.

Finally, I must acknowledge my sister, Linda Stevens. Linda has been a great encouragement to me. Every time I wrote a new poem or song, God told me to call Linda. I would be excited for her to hear what God had blessed me with. Linda was always a joyful sounding board. She has great insight into God's word and gave me helpful feedback. Through the years she has been tremendously supportive as a faithful prayer warrior and a loving friend. I thank God for my wonderful sister; her support was foundational in writing this book.

I could continue with more acknowledgments because my gratitude extends to many others. My family, close friends, and those who are part of my Christian walk are added to my list. However, let me simply sum up by saying, "Thanks be to God, the giver of all good things."

INTRODUCTION

Our God is truly amazing, and He can do anything. I, on the other hand, can do nothing worth doing on my own. All goodness comes from God because He is love and full of love. He saved me and placed a new heart within me, and that was over fifty years ago.

During this journey, whenever the valleys were so deep that I could only cry out to God or when the mountains were so high that I could only shout for joy, He would place beautiful words on my heart. It was His way of healing and giving comfort and bringing more joy and peace into my life at the most precious times of need. Some of the poems and songs were lost over time, sad to say, but as I grew older, I started writing them down and keeping them dear to my heart. I felt as though God wanted me to keep them for a reason.

Then one day, right out of the clear blue, God urged me to call a friend and read her two of my poems. I laughed to myself at this notion because she was a new friend I had just met at church. We clicked the moment we first talked. Her name is Suzanne, and she is a kindred spirit. God told me to call her and share my poems. I replied, "Lord, she'll think I'm crazy."

It seemed like a silly thing to do, but God has asked me to do silly things before, and I obey. So I picked up my phone and anxiously called Suzanne. She said the Lord had put me on her heart that morning, and she had been praying for me. She said God wanted her to pray because He had a message for me, and I needed to hear His voice.

"Well," I said, "the message must have been for me to call you and read you my poems." After sharing them with her, I explained how, at times, I thought I should publish what God had given me, but didn't have a clue where to start or where to go to make that possible. After I made that statement, she spoke up and said, "Judy, ask me what I do."

I was puzzled and said, "What do you mean?"

"You're not going to believe this," she repeated, "Ask me what I do."

"Okay, what do you do?"

"I publish books inspired by the Holy Spirit."

I had been out-mastered by the Master – again! – and knew immediately that God wanted me to have Suzanne publish the poems and songs He placed on my heart.

I don't claim to be anyone special. All glory, honor, and praise goes to Jesus, the only one worthy to pay the price. One thing I do know, from reading God's word and getting to know my Father, is that God desires for His children to know Him. He desires to be close to all His children.

My prayer is that after reading this book, you will be convinced that God wants to be in a close and loving relationship with you. He reveals Himself to those who truly seek Him.

❦ MY PRAYER ❦

Dear Heavenly Father,

Thank you for all the blessings and the goodness You bestow on Your children. I ask You to gently guide this book and place it in the hands of those who need it most. I pray for Your wisdom and guidance as I express this love from You. I want this book to encourage, uplift, and help open the eyes of those who may not know You. Lord, I pray that You will give them the comfort, the peace, and the joy that You so generously gave me as this book was being put together.

As always and forever, all glory, honor, and praise goes to You.

In Your most precious, beloved son's name, Jesus' name.

Amen and Amen.

He's Our Lord

*A*s a child learning to read my Bible, I loved the psalms. I guess that's because they were easier to read than the other books of the Bible. I discovered at a young age how it made my heart fill with joy and happiness to read such beautiful words that made my soul want to sing.

How fitting that God would bless me with a psalm of love to write and sing for Him. This song was written when I heard one of the musical pieces my brother-in-law sent me. My prayer is that you will read and enjoy the awesomeness of our God. How mighty is our God! He is our Lord!

"My prayer is that you will read and enjoy the awesomeness of our God."

He's Our Lord

GREAT ARE THE WORKS OF OUR LORD
    Holy is His precious name.
All nature sings of His love
    Glory to His name.
Come see the majesty of His power from above
    All nature sings of His grace and love.

To the tips of the highest mountains,
    to the pits of the deepest seas,
    His love will forever endure.
To the heavens above,
    to the earth here below,
    His love is forever more.

He's our LORD
    He is the Almighty God
He's our LORD and King,
    Proclaiming His praises; owing Him everything.
He's our LORD and God
    He is the reason that we sing.
Every knee shall bow and tongue confess
    that He is LORD and King.
Everything that has breath will shout and proclaim
    He is our reigning King.

Yes, to the tips of the highest mountains,
    to the pits of the deepest seas,
    His love will forever endure.
To the heavens above,
    to the earth here below,
    His love is forever more.
    He's our LORD.
    He's our LORD.
    He's our LORD.

I've Got Joy

Many years ago I was in a deep and dark valley. Things in my home were out of control. I had a husband who was angry most of the time. I had two teenagers with health and depression problems. I had just spent a sleepless night, crying and frightened, not knowing where my fifteen year old son had been for the past several nights. He and his father had a terrible fight that caused my son to run away like he had done several times before. The return of that cycle with her brother just made my daughter withdraw further and want to start cutting herself again. This was coupled with her skipping school.

My husband started screaming at me about how everything was my fault, and he slammed the door on his way out to work. I was crying and trying hard to control myself as I was getting ready for work. I started praying for God to help me find His peace in the situation and give me joy, hope, and strength to make it through one more day.

It's so amazing how God works in our lives. One would think He would place a sad song within me because of my frame of mind.

But it is just the opposite with God. He blessed me with a JOYFUL song, one I still sing today when I need to cheer up. Joy is one of God's spiritual fruits. He wants us to have a joyful spirit at all times.

"It's so amazing how God works in our lives."

I've Got Joy

SINCE I GAVE MY HEART TO JESUS,
My life has not been the same.
He has placed a joy deep within me;
I love to praise His name.
Through all my trials and all my good times,
I know Jesus walks with me.
And my joy is overflowing
Because I was blind but now I see.

It was grace that saved a lost soul like me
When I heard that old, old story
About a Savior from Calvary.
Now Jesus is my LORD forever;
Yes, Jesus is my victory.
I've got joy that's overflowing;
He took my place upon that tree.

I've got joy that's overflowing,
I've got joy down in my soul,
I've got joy over all my sorrows,
I've got joy over all my woes.

I will praise my LORD each morning,
I will praise until the sun goes down
Because I've got joy that's overflowing,
Yes I've got joy, joy, joy all around.

My Ultimate Cure

I woke up one day and realized I had been transported from a life full of hurt and pain to one full of love and forgiveness.

My first marriage had been a broken and torn up mess; it was never what it should have been. Agony and heartache were all I remembered about it. Then a beautiful thing happened: God blessed me with a wonderful man who knew how to love unconditionally. My new marriage was part of my fresh start. I was still battered, broken, and hurt. I had trust issues and was afraid of being wounded again.

My new marriage was a safe place for me to learn how to love and be loved. God gave me a man who could both love and forgive, and Tim showed me how. I needed God's healing, and He healed me with tender love and mercy through Tim.

During this time, God showed me the beautiful story of this woman in the Bible who needed healing too. She needed it physically and spiritually.

Our God heals completely. Are you in need of healing? God is here for you. He is our Heavenly Father and only wants what is best for His children.

"Our God heals completely."

My Ultimate Cure

For twelve long years my body was sick
    and there was no cure.
I had spent all I had on doctors
    how much more could I endure?
I was homeless, sick, and hungry
    and that day might have been my last.
Wait, what did I hear?
    It was a crowd coming fast.

I heard people shouting, "Jesus!"
    They kept calling out His name.
I had heard of all the stories
    and the spreading of His fame.

Then a hope rose within me as I thought about this man.
    He can walk on water, heal the diseases of the land.
I knew within my heart, He was the only hope now.
    I needed this Jesus. I had to get to Him, but how?

Suddenly, I thought, one touch was all I needed.
    Oh God, I cried out, get me through this crowd I pleaded.
And then as if by some miracle
    there He stood, His back to me.
The warmth and the love I felt
    drove me to my knees.

I knew He was my answer.
    He could save me, this I knew.
But a Jewish woman touching a man,
    they could put me to death if I do.
But what did I have to lose?
    I was already dying from within.
I needed to do it quickly;
    He wouldn't pass this way again.

And there upon my knees
    amid that very large mob,
I held on to all my faith
    as I touched the hem of God.
Never had I felt such joy;
    it was His power that's for sure.
In that touch I was healed;
    Jesus became my ultimate cure.

Quickly He looked around.
    Who touched Him, He wanted to know.
I knew I was no longer hidden,
    caught in the crowd before I could go.

With fear and trembling and falling to the ground
    I proclaimed my wonderful healing to everyone around.
Then Jesus looked at me,
    His eyes so full of love.
In that moment I knew
    He was my Messiah from above.
Softly He said, as He quickly turned to go,
    Be of good comfort, my daughter,
Your faith has made you whole.

This beautiful account is found in Matthew 9:20-22, Mark 5:25-34, and Luke 8:43-48. I wrote this poem as God unfolded the story right before my eyes. God inspired these words to retell the miracle.

The Father wants His children to know He is still performing miracles daily. We only need Jesus to help open our eyes to His handiwork.

"The Father wants His children to know He is still performing miracles daily."

A Lamb

It has always been a mystery to me how anyone can read the Holy Scriptures and not know who Jesus is. How can they deny Him? From Genesis to Revelation, the Scriptures point to Jesus. From the manger to the cross to the empty tomb, all Scripture is fulfilled in Jesus.

Yet there are so many who are blind and cannot see the words of truth. My prayer today is for the veil to be ripped open and for the blind eyes to see. Can you see a lamb? Do you know this lamb who can wash away your sin?

"Do you know this lamb who can wash away your sin?"

A Lamb

A STAR SHOWN BRIGHT ON THAT COLD, DARK NIGHT
    A gift from above, full of grace, full of love
A lamb who in that manger did lay
    A lamb who can take our sins away

He was born in Bethlehem
    He's the Great I AM
Promised seed of Abraham
    Bright and morning star
Savior to us all
    One who gives us life forever more

A lamb that came from above
    A lamb who is the perfect son of God
A lamb that is pure and holy from within
    A lamb, the only price to pay for our sin

Jesus was born in Bethlehem
    Jesus is the Great I AM
Jesus is the promised seed of Abraham
    Jesus is the bright and morning star
Jesus is the Savior for us all
    Jesus is life forever more

Jesus is the lamb that came from above
    Jesus is the lamb who is the holy son of God
Jesus is the lamb that takes away our sins
Jesus is a lamb
    A lamb

I Eloise Jesus

Isn't it good to know God loves speaking to His children? God is active, working to get our attention every day. We, however, have a hard time tuning in to His word and listening to His voice calling us.

This poem came to me on one of those occasions when I wasn't tuned in. I was trying to love anything and everything to make myself feel better. I was down and troubled, in a broken-hearted time of my life.

When our hearts are broken and hurting, all we can think of is how we can stop the pain. I wanted to fill the hurt and emptiness with things I thought I loved. It was then the Lord spoke to my heart. He wanted me to guard against saying that I love so many things and to stop over-using the word love. I hope this rhyme touches you.

"God is active, working to get
our attention every day."

I Eloise Jesus

I LOVE ICE-CREAM! I LOVE THIS AND THAT!
    I love my new sweater!
I love your new shoes and hat!
    We toss the word "love" around
With most of our favorite things
    We love everything from movies to sports,
Our possessions,
    Our golden rings

This word has become so over used
    "Love" no longer has that special sound
And when we really need to use it
    The word "love" falls flat to the ground
Like when I say I love Jesus
    Take notice of what I said
When I say I love Jesus
    It's with my heart and not my head

One sunny day while I was dreaming
    An idea illuminated my sight
I will make a new word that shows
    I love Jesus with all of my might
This new word is "Eloise"
    It has a beautiful sound to me
And can only be used to say I Eloise Jesus or God
    Or the Holy Spirit, you see

Where did I come up
    With "Eloise" you may say
Well God gave it to me
    On that bright and sunny day
And this new word has great meaning
    In its own special way

E stands for Exalted
    L is for true Love
O is for Overflowing
    I, an Immeasurable love from above
S is for Spirit-filled
    And **E** because it's Everlasting
    And wonderful and real

Now you know about my new word
    How I wish it could get a fresh start
Then whenever we say, "I Eloise Jesus!"
    It's special and loving from the heart

But maybe until a new word is made
    Or something more unique comes along
Perhaps we should not over use the word "love"
    The same old tune to the same old song

Open your hearts, God's children
    Let Him fill you from above
Save that word for what is pure and special
    Your Father can show you true love

I love love love love love love love love love love love love
love love love love love love love love love love love love love
love love love love love love love love love love love love love
love love love love love love love love love love

I love love love love love love love love love love love love
love love love love love love love love love love love love love
love love love love love love love love love love love love love
love love love love love love love love love love

I love love love love love love love love love love love love
love love love love love love love love love love love love love
love love love love love love love love love love love love love
love love love love love love love love love love

I love love love love love love love love love love love love
love love love love love love love love love love love love love
love love love love love love love love love love love love love
love love love love love love love love love love

I love love love love love love love love love love love love
love love love love love love love love love love love love love
love love love love love love love love love love love love love
love love love love love love love love love love

We use the word love for everything
from food to things to people to God.
It's no wonder we get confused about
the word love!

Sing Praises to You

I *was saved at the young age of five, and my life has been a constant walk with Jesus. He has always been with me. Through my darkest nights and most joyful events, Jesus has been there.*

I am not saying I have always been there for Him. It breaks my heart to say I have let Him down many times. I have made bad choices. I have done ugly things I am not proud of. But praise God, Jesus has been on my journey with me, always holding my hand. He guides, protects, corrects, encourages, and most importantly, He loves me. He places a true joy in my heart. He is my reason to live, and He is my inspiration.

*"He is my reason to live, and
He is my inspiration."*

Sing Praises to You

I COULD NEVER REPAY WHAT YOU HAVE DONE FOR ME
    but I can shine my light so the world will see.
How you saved my soul at Calvary
    You are the reason I want to sing.

The longer I've known You
    the more joy fills my soul.
You've given me a new song, changed my heart,
    and made me whole.
And I want to praise You as onward I go
    I want to sing love songs to You.

So if my heart wants to sing
    I will sing only unto You.
And if my heart wants to praise
    I'll praise You the whole day through.
You're the reason that I sing
    because You are my God!
You are my everything!
    I want to sing praises to You.

It Was Love

One sunny morning, while sipping my first cup of coffee, my brother-in-law Marvin called. He was bursting with excitement because he was writing music and wanted me to write the words. I had no idea he had such a gift! He said I could write words for him because I loved to sing for the Lord. He promised to send me a CD, and I couldn't wait for it to arrive.

When the music came, I was speechless as I listened to it - heavenly music that came straight from God. The first time I heard it, the only thing I could think of over and over was, "This is love." The only message I could hear inside my head was, "It is love." I knew it was love God wanted this music to express.

So became the title of Marvin's song, and so became the poem God gave me. I hope you enjoy the message of the song. To me, poems are songs, and songs are poems.

"I knew it was love God wanted to express."

It Was Love

IT WAS LOVE THAT MADE OUR SAVIOR WALK
    the road to Calvary
It was love that held Him there
    so from our sins we'd be set free
It was love that Jesus gave His life
    true love upon that tree

It was love that Jesus arose again
    It was love that set us free
It was love that conquered sin and death
    It was love, true victory
It was love that held Him to that cross
    It was love for you and me

It was love that made Him carry
    that cross for me and you
It was love that said forgive them
    for they know not what they do
It was love beyond all measure
    It was love pure through and through
It was love that held Him to that cross
    unconditional love for me and you

The Day I Washed Jesus' Feet

This is my favorite Bible story. I remember hearing it as a young girl and wishing I could meet Jesus. I wanted to wash His feet with my hair. Being young, I only thought about Jesus, her hair, and His feet; I didn't think about the woman's tears of repentance.

Yet it's because she cried so much that she was able to wash His feet. I wished I could too. As I grew older and faced many trials, I would reread this beautiful story, and each time God opened my heart to another part of it. I wouldn't remember reading the new part before, and yet it was my favorite account, so how did I miss these things? God reveals to us when we are able and ready to accept His truth.

I went through a painful separation and divorce several years ago and, at the time, I felt I would never again be whole. I didn't think I would be accepted or be able to serve in the church because of my being a divorcee. One evening I couldn't sleep and was trying to figure out what I should do about this mixed up life of mine. I started to cry, and I couldn't stop.

I opened my Bible and started reading this story again. God allowed me to visit the time and place as if I were there. He allowed me to write through my broken heart and see this woman in a new way. I hope you can visualize yourself in the room here with Jesus. I want you to sit down at Simon's table and witness one of the most loving acts toward our Lord and Savior.

The Day I Washed Jesus' Feet

I WOKE UP EARLY THAT MORNING
    Feeling lost and hopeless as before
All the guilt and shame I carried
    Cut through me to the core

I recalled Jesus would be visiting
    In our city that day
I believed He was the Messiah
    That's what the prophets say

He would be eating at the Pharisee's house
    Just over a block or two
I must be there to see Jesus
    He will tell me what to do

As I entered Simon's house
    I saw Jesus in front of me
I was frozen in that spot
    And I began to weep

My guilt and shame overtook me
    I could handle the pain no more
I stood and couldn't stop crying
    My tears falling upon the floor

As I knelt and begged for His forgiveness
    I started kissing His feet
I took out my only treasure:
    Priceless oil that smelled so sweet

My faith knew at that moment
    He could take my sins away
With the flooding of my tears and oil
    I washed His feet that day

The Pharisee, not understanding, said
    Why is Jesus just sitting there?
If He were a prophet He would know
    Who was washing His feet with her hair

Jesus looked at the Pharisee and said:

You gave me no water to wash dust from my feet
    You gave me no kiss as I came in from the street
You gave me no oil because of your fears
    Yet this burdened woman does so with tears

Because she loves me
    She washes dust from my feet
Because she loves me
    She anoints with oil so sweet

Because she loves me
    She shows kindness so rare
She continues to kiss my feet
    And dry them with her hair

And her sins, though many,
    Are forgiven her this day
Her faith in me made her whole;
    I take her guilt and shame away

When Jesus spoke these words of love
    My tears began to cease
He said, your faith has saved you
    Now you may go in peace

And so my story lives on forever
    Written words ever so sweet
Though my sins were many, with love and tears
    I washed my Savior's feet

Luke 7:36-50 is the biblical account of this wonderful story. Please take time to read it from the Bible. God always blesses His word. Get the full picture and understanding of what was happening on this special day. It is a beautiful picture of repentance and forgiveness.

*"God always blesses
His word."*

Put on the Armor of God

"*Finally, be strong in the Lord and in his mighty power. Put on the full armor of God, so that you can take your stand against the devil's schemes. For our struggle is not against flesh and blood, but against the rulers, against the authorities, against the powers of this dark world and against the spiritual forces of evil in the heavenly realms. Therefore put on the full armor of God, so that when the day of evil comes, you may be able to stand your ground, and after you have done everything, to stand.*

~ Ephesians 6:10-13

Put on the Armor of God

PUT ON THE ARMOR
Put on the Armor of God.
Your battle is not with flesh and blood
but the forces of evil.
The devil must retreat in the presence of the LORD.
Put on the Armor
Put on the Armor of God.

Gird yourself in Truth so you can stand
Keeping eyes on Christ and holding His hand.
Put on the Armor of God.

Hold up the Righteousness of God's Breastplate
While resisting all the attacks of evil and hate.
Put on the Armor of God.

Pick up the Sword of God's Holy Spirit
Sharing His love so the lost will hear it.
Put on the Armor of God.

Cover your feet with the Gospel of Peace
Then Satan's hold on you he must release.
Put on the Armor of God.

Daily wear the Helmet of Salvation
Sharing it with every tribe and every nation.
Put on the Armor of God.

Remember God's word is a light unto your feet
Speak His word and Satan must retreat.
Put on the Armor
Put on the Armor of God.

Your battle is not with flesh and blood
but the forces of evil.
The devil must retreat in the presence of the LORD.
Put on the Armor
Put on the Armor of God.

Get Behind Me, Satan!

*H*ave you ever had mornings when everything that could go wrong does go wrong? I was trying to get to church for prayer one morning, and every single thing I did blew up in my face: I couldn't find my shoes, my car keys were missing, the car at first wouldn't start, I drove half a mile before returning to grab something I forgot, AND I hit every red light on the way to the church!

I knew I would be ten minutes late, and was about to scream, when I threw my hands up in the air and yelled, "Get behind me, Satan! You have no hold on me! I belong to Jesus, and I am going to church to pray no matter what comes my way!"

Because I never knew when God would bless me with a song or poem, my husband Tim bought me a recorder to keep in my purse. I started singing and praising God in the car that morning. So the last half of this trip to church had me singing and telling Satan that he does not have a hold on me and recording it all the while!

The beautiful thing was when I finally arrived the morning prayer had been delayed – exactly ten minutes! So though I thought I'd miss the start, I didn't. With God's perfect timing, I was perfectly on time.

"With God's perfect timing, I was perfectly on time."

Get Behind Me, Satan!

Since I gave my heart to Jesus
    Satan just won't let me be
He tries to steal my light
    He doesn't want me to see
He wants to make me stumble
    Hurt others along the way
But in Jesus I have victory
    To Satan I do say

Get behind me, Satan
    You have no hold on me
Get behind me, Satan
    In Jesus there's victory
Get behind me, Satan
    From you I have no fear
Get behind me, Satan
    For Jesus is here

Every day life can be a battle
    On the outside and within
Satan tries to trick me
    He wants to make me sin
Then I pick up my Bible
    And its light shows me the way
When I shout out the name of Jesus
    The devil must run away

Get behind me, Satan. I have no fear
    Get behind me, Satan, for Jesus is here
And when Jesus is here all my doubts will flee
    He is my rock, my hope, my salvation
    He is my victory
Get behind me, Satan. From you I have no fear
    Get behind me, Satan, for Jesus is here

She is Only Asleep

Several years ago, we had a tragedy in our family - the death of a little one that was so hard to bear. Our young niece Audrey died in her sleep. It shook up the whole family. She was a healthy and happy two year old, and it came without warning. Her parents lovingly tucked her into bed one evening, and she was taken to heaven before morning arrived.

It was through this sad event and not understanding it that God blessed me with insight into another precious Bible story. In this one, Jesus shows us that He is the resurrection. He is the life. Through Him we will live forever.

"He is the life. Through Him
we will live forever."

Matthew 9:18-19, 23-26
Mark 5:22-24, 35-43
Luke 8:41-42, 49-56

She is Only Asleep

THE DAYS WERE LONG AND MISERABLE
    As our twelve year old daughter lay on her bed.
My husband denied she was dying,
    A crazy notion inside his head.

He believed in a man, a healer, a master,
    One called Jesus from Galilee.
He said, my dear I know He can heal her
    Just you wait and see.

Off he went to find Jesus; he'd bring Him back for sure
    Jarius' heart was so full of faith
Mine was hopeless,
    For there was no cure.

Hours lingered on as I watched our daughter
    I saw her breathe her last breath.
In my grief I cried, find my husband
    Tell him of our sweet daughter's death.

Meanwhile Jarius did see Jesus
    Gathered among many in the street.
My husband beseeched Him greatly,
    Falling down at Jesus' feet.

Sir, my little daughter is dying,
    She's at home upon her bed.
Come, lay your hands, and heal her,
    That is what my husband said.

Time is passing quickly, thought Jarius
    His heart beating faster and faster.
Then he heard, you're daughter is dead
    So no longer trouble the Master.

Jarius' eyes filled with tears
    He stopped and bent low.
Jesus said you must believe,
    She will be made whole.

When the two arrived, the house was crying
    And oh how they did mourn
When Jesus started talking of life
    The people laughed Him to scorn.

Why do you make such ado, He said
    And why do you weep?
This damsel's not dead
    She is only asleep.

Jesus cleared out the scoffers
    Then we entered her room.
Jarius and I fell to our knees,
    Our hearts so full of gloom.

Jesus took her by the hand and said,
    Little girl, arise.
We knelt there in astonishment
    As our daughter opened her eyes.

We shouted out for joy
    As she arose from her bed
She is alive! we proclaimed
    She is no longer dead!

I wanted to run and tell everyone,
    And that's when Jesus said,
Tell no man about the miracle here,
    Do not tell how she arose from the dead.

When something this beautiful happens,
    You know you've been set free.
It's a love story that can't be hidden
    You want the whole world to see.

Without Jesus all are lifeless and dead.
    All will morn and all will weep
But with Jesus, you will then hear Him say,
    She's not dead, she is only asleep.

Why is Your Faith so Weak?

Have you ever been badly injured? I was working in a day care early one morning, and the babies were arriving quickly. One of the infant's coats fell on the floor. I was in hurry and carrying a little one, and I slipped on the coat, holding the baby as close to me as I could. The child was okay, but I took a hard fall. My neck and back were damaged, and I was placed on bed rest. My healing was slow and painful. I declined the pain relievers the hospital prescribed because I was determined not to become addicted to any medication; I simply refused the risk. People I knew had been down that road when recovering from illness, and it wasn't for me.

It was during the difficult months of remaining in bed and relying on others that I began questioning my faith. I wanted God to heal me, and people were praying for me, but each day I seemed to get worse, and the pain was intense. I started believing I didn't have enough faith for God to heal me.

So not only was I hurting physically, I was beating myself up spiritually. God wasn't beating me up; I was doing it. One night when I was in difficult, serious pain, I cried out to God. I felt peace suddenly come over me; there was a warm sensation beginning at the top of my head, traveling down my whole body and going out through my feet. Peace, joy, and comfort were mine for the rest of the night; God had miraculously given me physical strength that night. Not then, and not since, have I needed subscription pain medication – yet another answered prayer.

"I started believing I didn't have enough faith for God to heal me."

Why is Your Faith so Weak?

HOW LONG MUST I BE WITH YOU BEFORE YOU UNDERSTAND?
The ways of my holy Father are not like sinful man.
I'm the Lamb, the perfect sacrifice,
I will fulfill my Father's plan.
You've seen my work and power,
When will you understand?

Oh foolish men, why is your faith so weak?
You watched me calm the troubled storm
By the words I speak.
You were with me when I fed the five thousand.
You saw me walk upon the sea.
Oh foolish men, why is your faith so weak?

I suffered and bled and died for the souls of men.
On the third day I arose and became
The ultimate price for sin.
There's evidence of my strength and power
Throughout this great big land.
Oh Christians, when will you understand?

Oh Christians, why is your faith so weak?
You've seen me calm the storms of your life,
I gave you inner peace.
I cleansed your heart and made you whole.
I laid your soul at my Father's feet.
Oh Christians, why is your faith so weak?

At the Well

Just as the physical needs water to survive, so does the spiritual. Jesus is the fountain of living water; He is the source of all life. We find over 1000 verses in Scripture describing many forms of water, and over half of these are about our Lord and Savior Jesus Christ.

The meeting between Jesus and the woman at the well (John 4:7-30) did not just happen. God had it all planned out. He knew the exact time to be at the well, and He knew all about this woman. He knew she was thirsty for the truth. He also knew she would get busy telling all who needed to hear about Jesus. He knew she would spend the rest of her life sharing her testimony.

The woman at the well willingly received and quickly went about doing what God wanted her to do. Like this woman, we also need to say, "Come let me show you the man who told me everything I ever did; is this not the Christ?"

We can't help but point to Christ. There are thirsty people all around us. If we don't tell them about Jesus, who will? Come and drink of this living water that will never go dry. When you drink this water, you will never die. Only Jesus promises to provide this water. Please come to Him, and live.

*"There are thirsty people all around us.
If we don't tell them about Jesus,
who will?"*

At the Well

ONE AFTERNOON I NEEDED COLD WATER
    My story I must tell
How I received God's living water
    The day I met Jesus at the well.

He looked tired, hot, and thirsty,
    Was waiting there you see
As I approached to draw my water,
    He lifted His head, then looked at me.

It was against the law to speak to Him,
    A Samaritan and woman the same
To Jews, we were low-life, disobedient,
    Full of dirt and shame.

He continued to look at me saying,
    Give to me a drink
And believing not my ears,
    I didn't know what to think.

I said, How can you, being a Jew,
    Even dare to talk to me
Right here in the middle of the day
    Where everyone can see?

He said, if you knew the gift of God,
    And who is speaking to you
You would ask for living water
    That's exactly what you would do.

I said, Sir, you have nothing to draw with,
    No bucket, no cup, no pail
Are you greater than our father Jacob,
    The one who gave us this well?

He said with living water,
    I will take your thirst away
And the water that I give to you
    Will spring to everlasting life this day.

Understanding not I asked for the water,
    Not wanting to come back to the well
He paused and said go, call your husband
    But I have no husband I did tell.

He knew I had had five husbands,
    He knew about my sin and shame
That day I met the Messiah
    Jesus Christ, His blessed name.

Forgetting about my water pot,
    I started shouting as I ran
I began telling everyone in the city
    About the meeting with this man.

It changed my life forever,
    That's why my story I love to tell
How I received God's living water
    The day I met Jesus at the well.

"Jesus answered "Everyone who drinks this water will be thirsty again, but whoever drinks the water I give them will never thirst. Indeed, the water I give them will become in them a spring of water welling up to eternal life."

~John 4:13-14

Roll Away That Stone

Sin is a big problem. That's why God sent an even bigger solution to take care of it. He sent His only begotten son to be the perfect sacrifice to atone for sin.

I was curious and wanted to know how many times the word sin was in the Bible. I found sin, sinned, sinnest, sinneth, and sinning. Using a concordance, I came up with 366 times. I may be a bit off, but at the time the number spoke volumes to me. I was struggling every day of the year, with sin trying to press in on me; 366 seemed fitting.

Praise the Lord that the blood of our precious Savior victoriously overcomes sin 24/7. We no longer have to be bound by sin. We just need to be bound to Jesus Christ who overcomes the sin problem. We choose Him.

"*Sin is a big problem. That's why God sent an even bigger solution to take care of it.*"

Roll Away That Stone

SIN IN YOUR LIFE CAN BE A BIG STONE
    That weighs you down
Sin can make you lifeless
    Old, dead bones walking around
Sin can steal your light
    Rob your joy from day to day
It's time to look to Jesus
    And roll that stone away

This world is full of sin
    And it will tear you down
Sin can take your laughter
    Turn your smile into a frown
Christians, don't let Satan
    Bind you up in a life of sin
It's time to look to Jesus
    It's time to live again

Roll that stone away
    You need help this very hour
Roll that stone away
    See God in all His power
Like Lazarus coming forth
    As Jesus called out to him
Roll away that stone!
    It's time to live again!

It's time to get on with your life
    It's time to be free from sin
Call out to Jesus
    It's time to live again

Just One Touch

"She said to herself, 'If I only touch his cloak, I will be healed.'"

~Matthew 9:21

This one verse shows the faith that brought about healing in this beloved story.

"Jesus turned and saw her. 'Take heart, daughter,' he said, 'your faith has healed you.' And the woman was healed at that moment."

~Matthew 9:22

Just One Touch

JUST ONE TOUCH IS ALL I NEED
    Just one touch will set me free
Just one touch from Jesus is all I need
    Just one touch will save my soul
Just one touch will make me whole
    Just one touch from Jesus is all I need

Because in His touch I find His power
    In His touch, His grace divine
In His touch He's full forgiveness
    In His touch there's peace of mind

Just one touch is all you need
    Just one touch will set you free
Just one touch will save your soul
    Just one touch will make you whole
Just one touch from Jesus
    Is all you will ever need!

Because in His touch you will find His power
    In His touch you will find His grace divine
In His touch you will find forgiveness
    In His touch you will find peace of mind
Just One Touch
    Is all you will ever need!

Jesus is the Only Way

The world has a problem with the statement that Jesus is the only way to heaven. People get upset because there is no other way. The world wants us to believe we are all working to get to the same place; we are on the same journey, we seek the same results. The world says all roads lead to heaven if we want to get there.

God's word tells us how to find salvation and everlasting life. There is only one way, and that is through God's only begotten son Jesus Christ. If you read about when God cleansed the world before, there was only one way to escape the destruction. And that was on the ark. There was only one ark. There was only one door. Therefore, there was only one way.

Keeping that same picture in mind, there is only one way to escape death and destruction, and that is through Jesus Christ. There is only one Jesus. He is the only door. He is the only way. Religious leaders from the time of Jesus until now are still in debate over this. People all over the world are being led to believe that there are several ways to get to heaven. My challenge to you, the reader, is to read and study God's word and ask the Holy Spirit to open your eyes to the full revelation of His word. He will show you the true way. If there were any other way, do you believe that God would have allowed His son to die if He did not have to? How crazy! Jesus would have died in vain.

Just picture this - Jesus is our ark. We need to accept Him and follow through the door into His body of protection. Remember one ark, one door. Don't be fooled like Galatia.

Jesus is the Only Way

In the Bible Paul warns Galatia:
    why are you such fools?
He tells them to throw away their laws
    and all their stifling rules

Galatia, you've been believing false teachers
    we've been told
That's why Paul stands and speaks
    so proud and bold

People, please heed Paul's warning
    if like Galatia you want the law
Because the just shall live by faith
    hope in good works cause man to fall

Jesus is the only way to salvation
    the law cannot pay for your sins
Jesus is the only way to glory
    good works won't get you in

God sent Jesus, the only way of salvation
    the law cannot pay for our sins
God sent Jesus, the only way to glory
    being good won't get you in

Jesus is the only way to salvation
    the law cannot pay for your sins
Jesus is the only way to glory
    going to church won't get you in

You Ask Me How

*T*his poem was given to me late one night after much prayer. I was struggling with how to reach my family.

Some want to debate and discuss God's word, but they are not asking honest questions from the heart. They want answers, but are unable or unwilling to, in faith, ask God for help.

It was after a long discussion with my son that I realized he was in this place – wanting answers but not stepping out toward God for himself. I was down and empty because I could not get him to understand or see. My heart was hurting because he couldn't believe that someone from long ago, whom he had never met, would die for him.

It was then the Holy Spirit said to me, "Don't talk to him any further. Be silent and pray for him to have faith to believe."

This happened several years ago, and I am still praying for my son's spiritual eyes to be opened. My prayer today is for all who read this poem, that their eyes will be opened, and they will ask for and receive the saving knowledge that Jesus is Lord.

"Some want to debate and discuss God's word, but they are not asking honest questions from the heart."

You Ask Me How

BORN IN MANGER A LONG TIME AGO
Lay a lamb who went to Calvary.
He came down from His home
So we can have life in Him.

He died and rose again to set us free.
You ask me how I know
These things are truly so.
You ask me how I know.

God so loved the world He gave us His son
So we can have everlasting life in Him.
And if you confess with your mouth, believe in your heart,
He saves your soul from within.

You ask me how I know
These things are truly so.
You ask me how I know
These things are true today.

I was lost in my sins, and Jesus took me in.
He saved my soul one day.
He put a song in my heart, a light in my path,
And He never will go away.

You see, I know. I know the LORD loves you so.
I know. Yes, I know *Jesus.*
You see, I know. I know Jesus can save your soul.
You just need to know.

You just need to know *Jesus.*
Know *Jesus.*

The First Stone

*H*ave you ever felt battered and bruised? Have you ever felt everyone's judgment around you because of something you did? It's hard enough going through trials without others casting stones, stabbing us in the back, and hurting us when we're already down.

When I was going through the worst time of my life, I felt so alone because the church wasn't there for me. There are some churches who wouldn't accept me now because I'm divorced. They likely wouldn't let me serve because I have "committed such a sin."

Jesus, on the other hand, does not condemn us. He loves and forgives us. There are loving and forgiving churches as well. They may be a little harder to find, but they are worth seeking out. There are loving men of God who are open to God's leading. God brought me to a church where I am a preschool director. God made a way for me to contribute. All have sinned, but thanks be to God; He will provide a way for anyone who seeks His face and wants to serve Him.

As we continue our journeys, others may pick up stones to throw. But Jesus and His true followers love us and won't condemn us for our mistakes and shortcomings. For we have all sinned, but praise God for sending His son to forgive. Jesus is the only one without sin. Notice that, in this Bible account, He could have thrown a stone, but didn't. He doesn't throw stones at us either. He just gives us His love and forgiveness.

The First Stone

THE MORNING WAS BRUTALLY INTERRUPTED,
    Shouts of angry men pounding my door.
The scribes and Pharisees were yelling,
    You will do this terrible thing no more.

I admitted I was a common adulteress,
    Caught up in the life I was leading.
I threw myself down at their feet,
    And for my life I was pleading.

Being thrown onto that terrible stage,
    My thoughts raced faster and faster.
The scribes yelled, take her to the temple
    And hand her to the Master.

My fears were overwhelming
    I was trying to be calm, not make a scene.
As they brought me to the one they called Master
    This Jesus, a carpenter, a Nazarene.

Master, they shouted, this is a woman of adultery
    Caught this very morning upon her bed.
Are we not commanded to stone her
    Is this not what the law of Moses said?

Wanting to tempt and accuse the Master
    These angry men gathered around.
But Jesus seemed not to hear them
    As He slowly stooped to the ground.

Time seemed to stand still
    And the silence did ever linger.
As all eyes were upon Jesus
    He started writing in the dust with His finger.

The accusing men kept asking
    About how the laws of Moses read.
Slowly the Master stood up
    And this is what He said.

He that is without sin
    Let him cast the first stone.
Jesus stooped down again, continued writing,
    The silence chilling to the bone.

One by one my accusers
    Started quietly walking away.
All the while Jesus was writing
    Something in the dust that day.

From the oldest scribe
    To the youngest Pharisee,
They were dropping their stones,
    The stones that were meant for me.

What happened next changed my life forever
    It was then I knew I was free.
Jesus asked, Woman, where art thou accusers?
    Hath no man condemned thee?

Looking to Him I said,
    No man, Lord.
Neither do I, said He.
    Go, and sin no more.

It was then Jesus became my Savior
    He saved my life that day.
Because Jesus being without sin
    could have thrown a stone my way.

But through Him there is no condemnation
    Through Him I will never walk alone.
Jesus could have been my Accuser
    Yet He loved me by not casting a stone.

This beautiful story is in the Gospel of John (Chapter 8, verses 1-11), and it's only recorded here. John was called the beloved, and his gospel is often called the love gospel. How fitting it is for John to be the one who records this picture of such a loving and forgiving Savior.

"John was called the beloved, and his gospel is often called the love gospel."

Within Time

*T*ime is a funny thing. When we are having fun, time flies by quickly. When we are having a difficult time, however, it drags slowly on. Seconds seem longer when we're in an uncomfortable situation. We can stop and scratch our heads at this one because one second is still one second.

Keeping this concept in mind makes it easier to understand how God's time and our time are two different things. We try to put timeframes on God's schedule when we can't understand His time at all.

We are to stand on His promises and believe that what He says He'll do is exactly what He will do. We are not to worry about when those promises will be delivered. God sends help at the precise time. He is never late.

He is the maker of time. He is the first, and He is the last. Rest assured that He holds time in His hands. Within time we will be going home to be with Him. Enjoy the journey, and don't worry about when things are going to happen - just know within time all things will be made new.

"God sends help at the precise time."

Within Time

WITHIN TIME, JESUS WILL TAKE US HOME.
    Within time, we'll march around His throne.
Within time,
    Within time,
Within time, we'll all go home.

Within time, He'll drive our tears away.
    Within time, night will turn to day.
Within time,
    Within time,
Within time, He'll drive our tears away.

Within time, we'll lay our troubles down.
    Within time, we'll wear a robe and crown.
Within time,
    Within time,
Within time, we'll lay our troubles down.

Within time, Jesus will take us home.
    Within time, we'll march around His throne.
Within time,
    Within time,
Within time, we'll all go home.

Your Final Hour

One of the greatest things about knowing Jesus as our Savior is we don't have to fear death anymore. Death is no longer a mystery. When we know Jesus, we know where we are going when we step through that door to the other side.

I love life, and I want to live a long, rewarding one serving Jesus and enjoying many blessings here on earth. But if today is my last day, I will be most happy to go home and see my Lord and all the loved ones who are in heaven too.

I don't mean to scare anyone, but the truth is that none of us knows when we'll take our final breath. They are two destinations afterwards. If you don't know yours, please prepare for what will come. Everything living on this earth must die. Death - the result of sin and the curse of Adam; only Jesus was able to break the chains. Please get yourself ready before it's too late.

"One of the greatest things about knowing Jesus as our Savior is we don't have to fear death anymore."

Your Final Hour

THIS COULD BE YOUR FINAL HOUR
    This could be your last breath
Where will you spend eternity
    When you close your eyes in death?

There is one thing that's for certain
    We will all die that's for sure
This life is forever fleeting
    Death one day knocks at your door

Death is coming and you can't stop it
    Here's the choice you need to make
Call on Jesus and He will save you
    Or the Devil your soul will take

This could be your final hour
    This could be your last breath
Do you know where you will spend eternity
    When you close your eyes in death?

Sitting at Jesus' Feet

Nothing pleases me more than to think of heaven. You see, I believe in a happily ever after.

The happily ever after event is heaven:

Happily
Ever
After
Victorious
Everlasting
Never-ending

To me, the greatest thing about heaven is that Jesus is there. I can't wait to see Him. I want to sit down at His feet.

"The happily ever after event is heaven."

Sitting at Jesus' Feet

LAST NIGHT I HAD A DREAM I WENT TO HEAVEN.
My love ones were waiting for me.
But all I could think of was my blessed Redeemer
And sitting down at His feet.

Heaven is rich and full of splendor
With mansions bright on a golden street.
But the rarest place beyond all beauty
Is sitting down at Jesus' feet.

When I die I'm going to heaven,
To that fair land that's rich and free
And when I finally see my Jesus
I will bow down at His feet.

My friend, when you arrive in heaven
And you want to look for me
Just remember what I told you
I'll be sitting at Jesus' feet.

Heaven will be my home forever.
There I'll spend eternity
And throughout all the ages
I want to sit at Jesus' feet.
Yes, throughout all the ages
I want to sit at Jesus' feet.

A Tiny Seed

The two most uplifting times of the year for me are Christmas and Easter. I enjoy the Scriptures about Jesus' birth and death, His burial and, praise God, His glorious resurrection. I reflect on the events and try putting myself into the stories. God's words are alive, and He allows us to experience them over and over again so we can know the wonderful things Jesus has done for us.

One day while I was reading, God gave me insight into a little seed. God lovingly planted a seed that would grow up to be the tree on which His son would die. I thought about promises from Abraham's time. God did not allow Abraham to sacrifice His son; He told Abraham a sacrifice would be provided, and there was indeed a ram caught up in the thickets (Genesis 22:13). This Scripture also refers to Jesus.

While Abraham did not sacrifice his son, many years later God sacrificed His. I was told that where Abraham was to sacrifice his son Isaac is the same place where Jesus was sacrificed. In the story, God told Abraham where to sacrifice - take a look at the Bible maps to see if the two locations are in the same region.

Do you think there was a bigger plan? You better believe there was! While thinking on these wonderful revelations, I began to think about the tree upon which Christ was sacrificed.

That tree was a living part of God's beautiful creation. Its life was taken to make the cross. God lovingly watched that tree grow just as He watched His son grow. I hope you enjoy reading this poem as much as I enjoyed writing it.

A Tiny Seed

IT WAS A LONG TIME AGO
    When in a manger a baby did lay
At the same time, somewhere,
    A tiny seed fell to the ground that day

As God lovingly watched His little son
    Grow into a child
He looked down with care
    On the seed becoming sapling wild

The years passed as God saw
    His child becoming a man
And the little sapling became a big tree
    According to God's great plan

God's son Jesus was faithful
    His father He did obey
Jesus knew what must happen
    On that coming, dreadful day

God continued looking down
    At the plan He had begun
Jesus was arrested
    For being God's only begotten son

God sadly watched Jesus being beaten
    For all the world to see
He also watched a man in the distance
    Chopping down a certain tree

If this tree could have talked
    I know what it would say
I don't mind giving up my life
    For the son of God to have His way

It's a privilege and an honor
    To be part of something great you see
I'm blessed to have a loving God
    Sacrificed on a simple tree like me

God gave His only son
    Can we deny such great love?
Jesus did as His father commanded
    Now we have hope from above

Who would have thought such a great act
    Would have a lowly, humble start?
It all began with a manger
    And a tiny seed playing its part

Just a thought:

When Jesus was born He was placed in a manger - a wooden box some believe. And when He gave up His life, He was placed on a tree.

He was born into a dead creation (manger)
He died for a dead creation (cross)
But He arose to give life anew (Resurrection)

"He died for a dead creation."

Apple of My Eye

God gave me this song one day when I was thinking about my Lord and Savior. After I finished, I had a memory resurface from nearly fifty years ago.

When I was eight, my older sister Joyce wrote a song about her first love. In it she called her boyfriend the apple of her eye. When this memory resurfaced, I phoned Joyce to share with her my new song. She did not remember writing a song about the apple of her eye years earlier. She laughed when I told her about it.

Since writing this song I came across a verse in the Bible: "Keep me as the apple of your eye; hide me in the shadow of your wings" (Psalm 17:8). God loves us and we are the apple of His eye. We are never out of His watch care or sight. What a beautiful picture this is. I spoke to Joyce recently, and she agrees.

"We are never out of His
watch care or sight."

Apple of My Eye

WHEN I WAS A YOUNG GIRL
Jesus saved my soul
He walks with me daily
He goes wherever I go
And now that I'm older
Life passing me by
Jesus is still the apple of my eye

Jesus is my first love
He is my best friend
He's preparing a place for me
When my journey here does end
And when this life is over
And I'm at home up in the sky
He will still be the apple of my eye

Jesus will always be the apple of my eye
He saved my soul and made me whole
In Him I'll never die
With Him I'll live forever
In that sweet by and by
He will always be the apple of my eye

There is More

Growing up in church, I learned many songs about heaven. What always bothered me about these songs is that they focused on heavenly "things" like gold streets and rubies. If the songs weren't about the stuff, then they were about how much better our lives would be when we got there (no pain, no problems, and so on).

But when I think of heaven, my first thoughts are about Jesus. I long to go to heaven because I want to see Jesus. I don't care what heaven looks like; I don't care where it's located or about the things that may or may not be there. I just want to see Jesus and know I will be with Him forever.

So there indeed is more. There is more than all the beauty and wonders. There is the One who is worthy. There is the One who deserves all honor and praise. Worthy is the lamb who was slain. Heaven to me is just one word - Jesus!

"I long to go to heaven because I want to see Jesus."

There is More

I SING ABOUT MY HOME ON HIGH
    About a land sweet by and by
I dream about my treasures there
    Can't wait to see that land so fair

I sing about a robe and crown
    Those pearly gates, I'm heaven bound
Big mansion there awaits for me
    In the sweet by and by forever I'll be

But there is more than the streets of gold
    The crystal sea, mansions to behold,
It's God's own son, my greatest gift to see
    My Jesus Christ, the one who died for me.

Jesus is all I'll ever want
    Jesus is all I'll ever need
I will live with Him
    Throughout eternity

Whatever You Sow

I enjoy the country and the open fields of crops growing in the sunshine. A small seed is planted, and lo and behold a large plant with good fruit grows. All the right conditions are needed for the good plant and fruit to come about.

God's word tells us in Galatians 6:7-8: "Do not be deceived: God cannot be mocked. A man reaps what he sows. Whoever sows to please their flesh, from the flesh will reap destruction; whoever sows to please the Spirit, from the Spirit will reap eternal life."

Notice that the word Spirit is capitalized. That's because the Spirit is Jesus Christ. Notice what we will reap if we sow to please Jesus - life everlasting.

"Notice what we will reap if we sow to please Jesus – life everlasting."

Whatever You Sow

WHATEVER YOU SOW IS WHAT YOU WILL REAP.
Your reward is just;
God's word He will keep.
Watch what you say,
Watch what you do,
Whatever you sow will come back to you.

God's holy word tells you time and again
How to live your life, stay away from sin.
It doesn't take much wisdom to know
That you will reap just what you sow.

Life can be hard in this world below,
Choices we make as onward we go.
If it's love you want, love you must sow.
Sow seeds of love, and watch it grow.

Whatever you sow is what you will reap.
Your reward is just;
God's word He will keep.
Watch what you say,
Watch what you do,
Whatever you sow will come back to you.

Think on These Things

"*Do not be anxious about anything, but in every situation, by prayer and petition, with thanksgiving, present your requests to God. And the peace of God, which transcends all understanding, will guard your hearts and your minds in Christ Jesus.*

"*Finally, brothers and sisters, whatever is true, whatever is noble, whatever is right, whatever is pure, whatever is lovely, whatever is admirable—if anything is excellent or praiseworthy—think about such things.*"

Philippians 4:6-8

Think on These Things

GO TO GOD'S WORD, AND READ IT EACH DAY.
It will help you know what to do and say.
It will bring you joy. It will make you sing.
If you will think, think on these things.

God's Holy Bible is here for you.
It brings you hope,
Makes your life brand new.
It will light your path; oh, the joy it will bring
If you will think, think on these things.

Whatever is good. Whatever is pure.
Whatever is good. Whatever is pure.
Whatever is good. Whatever is pure.
Our Heavenly Father says think on these things.

Think on these things when you feel life has got you down.
Think on these things when you feel you can't turn around.
When there is no other place to go,
Remember who is in control.
Our Heavenly Father says think on these things.

Whatever is true. Whatever is honest.
Whatever is just. Whatever is pure.
Whatever is lovely. Whatever is good.
Our Heavenly Father says think on these things.
Our Heavenly Father says think on these things.

About Judy

Judy Boggs grew up in Illinois, the twelfth of thirteen children. She was saved when she was five years old, and has spent her life walking with and getting to know the Father, His beautiful son, Jesus, and the Holy Spirit.

Judy taught schoolchildren for a number of years and has used her gifts and talents to serve in many churches. She currently resides in Kentucky with her husband, Tim. They have four children and ten grandchildren.

Inspiring Words to Rhyme is her first book.

www.ingramcontent.com/pod-product-compliance
Lightning Source LLC
Chambersburg PA
CBHW082005060426
42449CB00036B/3329